What makes things
Move?

Library of Congress Cataloging-in-Publication Data

Althea.
    What makes things move? / by Althea; illustrated by Robina Green.
       p.   cm.—(First science)
    Summary: Discusses how both living and non-living things move or
are moved.
    ISBN 0-8167-2124-6 (lib. bdg.)   ISBN 0-8167-2125-4 (pbk.)
    1. Motion—Juvenile literature. 2. Force and energy—Juvenile
literature. [1. Motion. 2. Force and energy.] I. Green, Robina,
ill. II. Title.
QC73.4.A47 1991
531'.11—dc20   90-10924

Published by Troll Associates, Mahwah, New Jersey 07430

Copyright © 1991 by Eagle Books Limited

Printed in the U.S.A.

10 9 8 7 6 5 4 3 2 1

What makes things
Move?

Written by
Althea

Illustrated by
Robina Green

Troll Associates

Wiggle your fingers.
Wriggle your toes inside your shoes.
Roll your eyes.
Blink your eyelids very fast.
You tell your brain to make
all parts of your body move.

Can you wiggle your ears?
You may have to think very hard
to use the right muscles to
make your ears move.

5

Can you remember how you
got around before you could walk?
Babies soon learn to move about.
Some crawl, others push themselves
on their bottoms.
Now, using your legs,
you can walk, jog, or even run.

It takes energy to move.
We get our energy from eating food.
We breathe in oxygen. Then the oxygen
mixes with the food we eat
to make fuel.
Fuel gives us the energy
we need to move.

Do you know why you breathe
faster when you run?
You need the extra oxygen
to give you more energy.

If you want to move faster,
you need wheels.
Bicycles can move fast.
They have two wheels.
You push on the pedals to make
the wheels go around.
If you pedal fast, you can move
more quickly than you can run.
Your energy makes the
bicycle move.

9

Motorbikes and cars go
much faster than bicycles.
They have engines to turn
their wheels.

The engines burn fuel
to give them energy.
Their fuel comes from
a gas pump.

Animals don't have wheels,
but many of them can move faster
than we can.
Ostriches can't fly,
but they have two powerful legs
for running.
Ostriches run even faster
than you can go on your bike!

A kangaroo doesn't run.
It hops on its two back legs,
and moves as fast
as an ostrich.

Most animals use more
than two legs to move along.
The cheetah, with its four legs,
can sprint faster than any
other animal.
But it can't keep going
that fast for long.
It would take too much energy.

So the cheetah creeps along,
stalking its prey until it is
quite close. Then it runs
very fast to catch its dinner.

Ducks rock from side to side
as they waddle along
on two legs.
They can't move fast on land.
Their legs are made for
swimming and their wings
for flying.

Have you ever been in
a rowboat?
The oars push against the water
to make the boat move.
Ducks and swans row with
their legs to move
swiftly through the water.

Can you swim?
To swim, you use your arms
and legs like the oars of
a rowboat.
They push you through the water.

Fish swim under the water.
They wiggle their fins and
beat their tails from side to side
to drive themselves
through the water.

Blow up a balloon
and let it go.
The air shoots out as it
whizzes through the air
like a rocket.

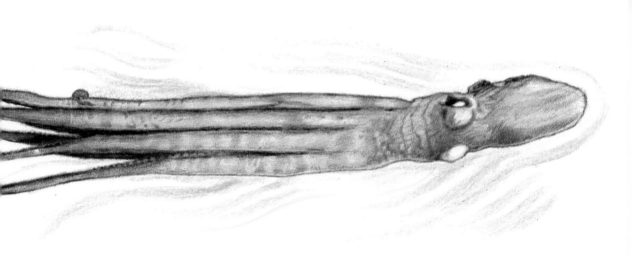

Octopuses and squid use
their arms like legs
to creep along the bottom
of the sea.
But to move quickly, an octopus
or squid sucks in lots of water and
then squirts it out very fast
through a small hole.
This drives it rapidly through
the water, just like a jet engine
or just like the balloon whizzing
through the air.

Wind is moving air.
We can use wind to make
things move.
Sailboats need wind
to drive them through the water.
The rudder at the back
is used to steer the boat
so it moves in the
right direction.

The wind turns the sails
of a windmill.
When there is no wind,
the sails stop going around.

Windmills were used
to grind wheat to make flour.
Now people build windmills
to make electricity.

Kites need wind to keep
them flying in the sky.
When the wind stops blowing,
they fall to the ground.

Birds don't need wind.
They flap their wings to
fly through the air.
But when they are high in the air,
they can use the wind
to glide or soar.

Don't you wish you could
fly like a bird?

25

Instead of flying like birds,
we can fly in airplanes.
Airplanes have powerful engines
to make them move very fast.
The air rushing over their wings
lifts them off the ground.

Blow gently on the piece of paper,
and it will lift like a wing.

Airplane wings are designed to fly.
But airplanes are heavy and
they need engines to lift them up.
The engines burn fuel to
give them the power to drive
the airplane through the sky.

All movement uses energy
or gravity.
Gravity is the earth's
downward pull that makes
things we drop fall to the ground.

Heat is a form of energy.
Wind gets its energy
from the heat of the sun.

Most machines burn fuel
to give them energy to move.
People and animals eat
food for fuel to give them
energy to move.

If you are traveling
in an airplane or a car
or a train, you know you are
moving.
You can see the world going
by outside.
You may be able to feel
the movement.

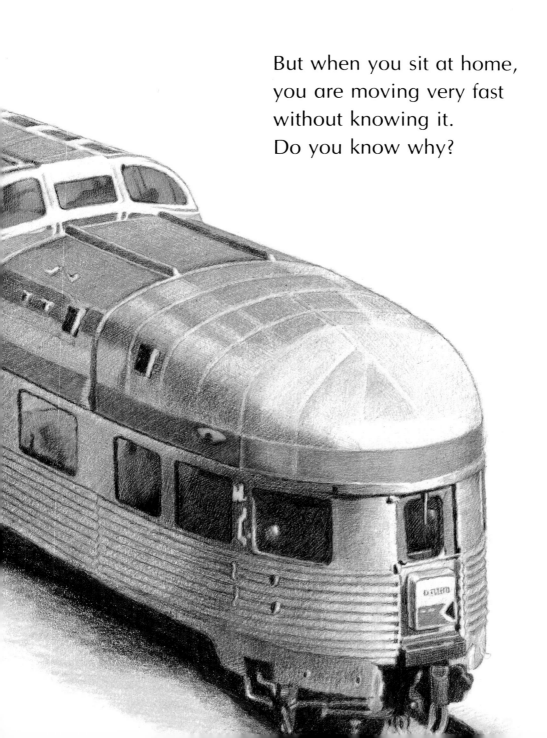

But when you sit at home,
you are moving very fast
without knowing it.
Do you know why?

The earth we live on spins
around at about 1,000 miles
an hour!